52

ICE
BREAKERS

52 ways to get to know your youth group

Day One

© Day One Publications 2012
First printed 2012
ISBN 978-1846253287

9 781846 253287

ISBN 978-1-84625-328-7
British Library Cataloguing in Publication Data available

Published by Day One Publications
Ryelands Road, Leominster, England, HR6 8NZ
Telephone 01568 613 740
FAX 01568 611 473
email—sales@dayone.co.uk
web site—www.dayone.co.uk
North American e-mail—usasales@dayone.co.uk
North American web site—www.dayonebookstore.com

Design by Rob Jones
Printed by Orchard Press Chetenham Ltd

52 Icebreakers

Many of these icebreakers have been handed down through generations of youth workers, adapted, changed and re-used; I've learnt many of them from watching others. You may notice a slight variation in the rules to the ones you already know, the great thing is, you can adapt them to suit your own circumstances.

Why use Icebreakers?

Often, when you bring together a new group of children/young people – or even adults, it can be hard to get them to integrate and chat. They naturally migrate to people they know. Icebreakers play an important part in helping to get young people to connect with each other in a group setting. It is a great way to involve the shy and quieter ones as well as encouraging team play with each other. It also promotes listening, cooperation and social skills.

Another interesting way of using icebreakers is by connecting them to the talk by way of a theme.

When using Icebreakers ...

- ✓ Be enthusiastic
- ✓ Don't embarrass anyone
- ✓ Don't persist, if it's not working – move on
- ✓ Make sure it's fun
- ✓ Stop before it ceases to be fun
- ✓ Only use one or two for each session
- ✓ Vary the ones you use

Contents

For Karla Mickelsen –
with thanks for your friendship
and encouragement

01 3 in 10

Instructions

- The leader needs to think in advance of a list of People, Places and Things

- Take the first group member and tell them a word from each of the categories, they then have 10 seconds to make a sentence which incorporates all of those words

- Repeat for all team members giving each different words

Items required

☐ Prepare a list of people, places and things

02 5Cs

Instructions

- Hand a piece of paper to each group. They must write down their favourite
  - Colour
  - Cuisine
  - Country
  - Chocolate
  - Car
- Write their name on the card and return to the leader
- Hand out another piece of paper to each in the group
- As the leader reads out the answers, they must guess who said it
- The one with the most right answers wins

Items required

☐ Pens
☐ Paper

03 5 Words

Instructions

- Split the group into teams of about four

- Give all the teams the same topic and give them 3 minutes to come up with five words they associate with that topic

- For every original word (i.e. one the other teams haven't got) they get a point

Items required

- [ ] Prepare a list of topics

04 An epic tale ...

Instructions

- Bring in advance enough objects so that everyone gets one. They need to be different and unconnected

- Put them in a bag and get each person to pull one out

- The leader begins to tell a story. As you go round the room each player must incorporate their object into their part of the story

Items required

☐ One object for each team member

05 Baby time

Instructions

- Each leader needs to submit a baby photo of themselves

- Stick them up around the room with no names

- The group must then match the leader to the photo

Items required

☐ One baby photo of each leader

06 Bible name scramble

Instructions

- Write out a list of 20 Bible names, scrambling the letters
- Give each team the 20 names
- The first team to accurately unscramble them wins

Items required

☐ List of 20 scrambled Bible Names

07 Charades down the line

Instructions

- This is a combination of Charades and Chinese Whispers

- Each person must act something simple to the person next in line, they then repeat to the person next to them and so on down the line until each person has had a turn

- Get the final person to act it out in front of everyone

- Then get the first person to perform the original – compare the difference!

Items required

☐ None required

08 Counting fingers

Instructions

- Divide your group into pairs, and get them to face each other

- Each person holds up their choice of number of fingers behind their back

- On the count of three each one pulls their hands from behind their back

- The first person to correctly add up the number of fingers held up by both wins

Variation – run this as a championship, winner plays winner etc.

Items required

☐ None required

1, 2, 3...

09 Crash

Instructions

- Get the group to move around the room without stopping

- When the leader shouts a number people must get into groups of that number

- Any group which does not succeed is out

Items required

☐ None required

10 Cross if you ...

Instructions

- Sit everyone on chairs in a circle

- Have one person stand in the centre

- The centre person must name something they have done i.e. 'cross if you have ever been on a plane'

- The people who answer 'yes' must cross the room to the seat of someone else who says 'yes'

- The last person left stays in the middle and chooses the next 'cross if ...'

- After three times in the middle that person is out

Items required

☐ None required

11 Draw your name

Instructions

- This only works for groups who don't know each other

- Put people in pairs, each pair must reveal their name to the other one only by drawing

- No other communication is allowed

Items required

- ☐ Scraps of paper
- ☐ Pens

12 Face to face

Instructions

- Put your group into pairs
- The group leader will shout out a topic which the pairs must then discuss for 30 seconds
- Then switch partners and give out a new topic
- Replay as many times as you like
- Try to choose interesting topics such as 'if you were stuck in a bus with anyone from history, who would you like it to be?'

Items required

☐ List of topics

13 Find someone who ...

Instructions

- Give everyone a sheet listing the categories

- Each player must find someone whose name they can write down next to each category

- Players may only use each person once

- Players cannot write down the name of someone who isn't present or use themselves

- Use categories like

    Has more than two brothers

    Likes Chinese food

    Has never seen a whole football match

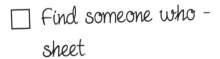

Items required

☐ Find someone who - sheet

14 Finding twins

Instructions

- Prepare ahead of time your category such as animals, famous people, occupations, emotions, sports, etc.

- Write the same thing twice on different pieces of paper

- Hand out the paper. People should not tell anyone what is written down

- Each player must find their twin by making a noise/action associated with their name

Items required

☐ List of items

15 Flags

Instructions

- This does not have to be long. Emphasise, neat artwork is not the aim! I suggest putting a time limit on this

- Give each person a piece of paper and pencil crayons

- Have them design a flag which they feel best represents themselves

- They must then show the group and explain why

Items required

☐ Scraps of paper
☐ Pens

16 Guess the voice

Instructions

- Seat everyone in a circle
- Blindfold one person
- Seat the blindfolded person at the feet of someone on a chair
- The person on the chair then makes a meow noise
- The blindfolded person must then guess who is making the noise

Items required

☐ None required

Meeeeooooow!

17 High fives

Instructions

- Stand in a large circle and ask a question

- If the answer is 'yes' people must run to the centre of the room, jump in the air and high five each other, then return to the circle

- Suggested questions

    Have you ever eaten frogs' legs?

    Have you ever been abroad?

    Have you ever broken a bone in your body?

    Have you ever moved house?

Items required

☐ None required

18 Hug a balloon

Instructions

- Select six people and put in pairs – make sure they are comfortable with this!

- Give each pair 3 balloons

- After the leader shouts 'go' the pair must blow up their balloons, tie them off and place one under one person's armpit, one under the other person's and one between them

- They must hug each other until all balloons are burst

- The winner is the pair who is the quickest

Items required

☐ Pack of balloons

19 I like to ...

Instructions

- Seat everyone in a circle
- The first person begins with "I like to ..." (e.g. go walking)
- The second person says "Tirzah likes to go walking and I like to read"
- The third person says "Tirzah likes to go walking, Sam likes to read and I like to ..."
- Continue around the room until the final person has to say everything
- If a person gets stuck, get the rest of the group to help out by miming the activity

Items required

☐ None required

20 If

Instructions

- In advance write out 20 questions beginning with 'If' on index cards

    i.e.

    If you could go anywhere in the world, where would you go?

    If I gave you £/$10,000, what would you spend it on?

    If you could watch your favourite movie now, what would it be?

    If you could talk to anyone in the world, who would it be?

- Place the cards in the centre of the circle, face down

- Choose a player to choose a card and answer the question

- The next player selects a different card and so on until everyone has answered a question

Items required

- ☐ 'If' cards

21 Interview

Instructions

- Divide the group into pairs
- Ask them to take three minutes to interview each other
- Each interviewer has to find out three interesting facts about their partner
- Bring everyone back to together and ask everyone to present the three facts about their partner to the rest of the group

Items required

☐ None required

22 I've never ...

Instructions

- Sit the group in a circle holding up 10 fingers

- Go round the room getting each person to make a statement such as 'I've never been skiing'

- Anyone in the circle who has been skiing must put a finger down

- When you have no fingers left you are out

- Keep going until you have the 'last man standing'

Items required

☐ None required

23 Joke & punchline

Instructions

- Select a number of jokes
- Write the joke on one card and the punchline on another
- Mix the cards up
- Make sure you have enough cards for one for each person
- On the command, people must walk amongst the group trying to find the other half of their joke

Knock knock

Items required

☐ Joke cards

24 Links

Instructions

- Divide into pairs

- Ask each pair to sit on the floor with their partner, backs together, feet out in front and arms linked

- Each pair must try to stand up together

- To make it harder, join pairs together and work in a four and so on ...

Items required

☐ None required

25 Mingle and talk

Instructions

- This is a slightly more chatty version of 'Find someone who'

- Each person has a set of instructions to follow, they must then mingle to find the answers. Examples

    Count the number of blue eyed girls in the room

    Find out who has travelled the furthest on holiday

    Who has the most unusual hobby?

    Find the weirdest thing anyone has eaten

    Who knows what 'Hippopotomon—strosesquippedaliophobia' is a fear of?

Items required

☐ Instruction cards

26 My letter name sentence

Instructions

- Have each person describe him/herself by using the first letter of his/her name

- For example: My name is Tirzah and I like Tuna, my car is a Toyota and I play the Trumpet

Items required

☐ None required

27 Name chain

Instructions

- Choose one person to begin the chain
- For example, if the first person in the chain is Jonathan then the second person's name must begin with an N, for example Naomi, the next must begin with an I
- You have 5 minutes to make the longest chain you can

Items required

☐ None required

28 Name grid

Instructions

- Divide the group into groups of four (try to mix people with long and short names)

- Each group needs paper and pens

- Ask them to draw a grid on which they write their forenames. For example,

P	H	I	L	L
S	A	R	A	H
M	A	R	Y	
J	O	H	N	

- Give each team three minutes to write down as many words (three letters or more) that they can make only using the letters in their names

- Letters must adjoin each other in the grid, but do not have to be in a straight line

- After three minutes each team adds up their score

- 3 or 4 letter words = 1 point

- 5 letter word = 2 points

- 6 letter word = 3 points

Items required

- ☐ Pens
- ☐ Paper

29 One minute

Instructions

- In advance come up with a list of topics and write each on a card

- Place the cards in a bag

- Bring a member to the front of the room, they must dip their hand in the bag and choose a topic

- They must then talk for 1 minute on that subject – don't let them finish early or go on too long!

Items required

☐ Topic cards

30 Phobias answered

Instructions

- Prepare two sets of cards – one with the phobia listed and one with the description
- Hand two cards to each member in the group and have them exchange cards till they have a matching pair
- Some phobias are: - (many more can be found on the web)
  - Hippopotomonstrosesquippedalio—phobia - Fear of long words
  - Arachibutyrophobia - Fear of peanut butter sticking to the roof of the mouth
  - Alektorophobia - Fear of chickens
  - Ephebiphobia - Fear of teenagers
  - Amaxophobia- Fear of riding in a car
  - Chronomentrophobia- Fear of clocks
  - Lachanophobia- Fear of vegetables

Items required

☐ Phobia cards

31 Picnic time

Instructions

- Initially only the leaders should know how to play this game

- It is played by taking the first letter of your first name and the first letter of your surname, using those letters chose two items to take on your picnic. So for example Tirzah = Tomatoes. Jones = Juice.

- Start by stating you are going on a picnic and what you are going to take. For example "My name is Tirzah Jones and I am taking Tomatoes and Juice"

- Then move onto the next person, if they have not worked out the game, and get it wrong tell them they can't go on the picnic

- Keep going until all your group have worked out how the game is played

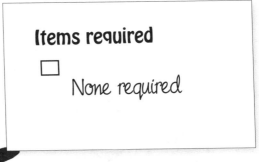

Items required

☐ None required

32 Pop the balloon

Instructions

- You need to come prepared with plenty of balloons and string

- Tie a balloon on a string (at least two feet long) to each person's ankle

- Your group must run around the room trying to pop each other's balloons while protecting their own

Items required

- ☐ Balloons
- ☐ String

33 Reactions

Instructions

- Prepare a number of cards in advance with an 'incident' written on it, for example

    'Winning a gold medal'

    'Falling off your bike'

- Get one player to stand in the centre of the circle and act out their reaction to what happened

- Other players must guess what the incident was

Items required

☐ Reaction cards

34 Roll the marble

Instructions

- Divide your group into two

- Seat them in two rows opposite each other

- Each person needs a cardboard insert from the centre of a kitchen roll/paper towel

- Hand a marble to the first player

- The marble must roll from one end of the row to the other, through the tubes in the fastest time possible

- If the marble gets dropped along the way then they must return to the beginning

Items required

☐ a cardboard insert from the centre of a kitchen roll/paper towel for each team member

☐ 2 marbles

35 Shoe pile

Instructions

- Have everyone remove their shoes and put them in a pile in the middle of the room

- Each person must then go and pick up a pair of shoes and try to find who they belong to

Items required

☐ None required

36 Silent lines

Instructions

- Choose a selection of things for your group in which they can order themselves. i.e. age, month of birth etc.

- Here is the catch, they must not speak to find out the information

Items required

☐ None required

37 Smarties

Instructions

- Buy a bag of smarties/'M&Ms' (or other coloured sweets)

- In advance work out what colours are in the bag and assign each colour a piece of information

    i.e.

    Red – Favourite hobbies

    Green – Favourite holiday destination

    Blue – Favourite memory

    Yellow -Dream job

    Orange – Wildcard (tell us anything about yourself!)

- Do not explain the game in advance, just hand out the smarties and ask each player to take one (not to be eaten)

- Write on the board what each one symbolises then go round the room finding out the information

Items required

☐ Bag of Smarties (or other coloured sweets)

38 Spider's web

Instructions

- Everyone stand in a circle
- The first player must hold one end of a ball of string and throw the ball to someone else as they ask a question
- After answering they hold the string and repeat the exercise
- Warning! you can get seriously tangled up!

Items required

☐ Ball of string

39 Steal the sticker

Instructions

- As the group arrives, place ten stickers on their backs and give them each a piece of paper

- The object of the game is to try and steal as many stickers as possible without getting caught or losing yours

- Whoever has the most wins

Items required

☐ Stickers

40 Stranded

Instructions

- Following a shipwreck, everyone has been stranded on a desert island!

- Each person can take one item with them

- However, the item must in some way represent them and be useful

- Get each person to say what they are bringing and why

- If you have time, split into groups of around five. Each group must then combine their items and come up with an inventive way of how they can increase their survival chances by taking all five

- Share with the whole group

Items required

☐ None required

41 Suddenly

Instructions

- Start off the game with a sentence. For example; "Yesterday I went to the beach and was walking past a life guard when SUDDENLY ..." the next person must take up the story ending their part with the word SUDDENLY until all the group have had a turn

Items required

☐ None required

42 Table topics

Instructions

- In advance prepare a selection of topics to discuss – suggestions:
    - Which piece of land would you wish to be preserved forever?
    - What's your favourite quotation?
    - Which song evokes the strongest memories for you?
    - If you could meet any footballer who would it be and why?
- Organize your group into smaller groups of about four and get them to discuss a variety of topics
- Each group must then report back on what they have learnt about each other

Items required

- ☐ Topic cards

43 Toilet roll

Instructions

- Hand around a toilet roll asking each person to take as many sheets as they want. Do not explain anything at this point

- When they have done this, get each person to give as many facts about themselves as they have sheets of toilet roll

- This only tends to work once!

Items required

- [ ] Toilet rolls

44 Unique and shared

Instructions

- Split the group into teams of about five, give them a pen and paper

- Each team must come up with something which is the same for everyone (avoid the obvious i.e. we all have hair)

- Secondly, think of a unique fact about yourself .... It has to be something that cannot be said about anyone else

- If they say something different from any other team they get points. Leaders need to be creative when it comes to scoring and the reason they give points

Items required

☐ Pen
☐ Paper

45 What's different?

Instructions

- Split your group into pairs, make sure they don't know their partners

- They have 1 minute to talk to each other

- They must then turn and stand back to back

- They have 1 minute to change five things about their appearance i.e. remove glasses etc.

- Turn them back round to face each other, they have 2 minutes to guess the changes

Items required

☐ None required

46 Whistle that tune

Instructions

- Sit the group in a circle

- Take one person to one side and whisper a well-known tune to them

- They must then whistle the tune to the rest of the group who must guess it. (If they really can't whistle you could get them to hum, but it makes it more fun if they can't whistle very well)

- Give everyone in the group an opportunity to go up to the front

- You may wish to prepare your tunes in advance

Items required

☐ None required

47 Who am I?

Instructions

- Write on post-it-notes a list of well known people/cartoon characters. One person per 'post it'

- Stick one on each person's back

- They must go round the room asking questions of everyone else to help find out who they are

Items required

☐ Post-it notes
☐ Character list

48 Who is it?

Instructions

- Have each person write a little known fact about themself on a piece of paper then hand it to the leader

- The leader shuffles them and then reads out each fact

- As the leader reads out the facts, everyone must guess who it is

Items required

- ☐ Paper
- ☐ Pen

49 Who moved first?

Instructions

- The point of the game is for a chosen player to figure out who started the motion that everyone is doing

- Sit the group in a circle

- One person is sent out of the room or out of sight of the group

- The leader silently points to one person in the group. That person is the motion-starter. They start a motion such as clapping their hands, rubbing their tummy etc.

- Once the motion is started, the person outside comes back and stands in the middle of the circle

- The motion starter can change the motion any time and as the other people in the circle see the motion change, they change too as quickly as possible

- The person in the middle has three guesses as to "who moved first?"

Items required

☐ None required

50 Whose feet/hands?

Instructions

- Divide your group into two teams and send one team out of the room

- Take a large sheet and have the rest lie underneath it with only their hands or feet showing (the leader chooses which and makes sure everyone is showing the same)

- Bring the rest back in, they must guess who the feet/hands belong to

Items required

☐ Large sheet

51 Wind and talk

Instructions

- Get a large ball of string and cut it into different lengths

- Bunch them up into your hand and have one player pull out a piece of string

- Have them wind it neatly around their finger

- As they are winding, they must talk about themselves without a break. If you don't think they are winding neatly enough you can make them rewind

Items required

- ☐ Ball of string
- ☐ Scissors

52 Would you rather ...

Instructions

- In advance prepare a list of 'would you rather' questions

Examples:

- Would you rather visit the doctor or dentist?

- Would you rather be able to fly or be invisible?

- Would you rather eat a banana or a pear?

- Place a line of tape down the middle of the room

- Ask the group to stand down the line one foot on either side of the tape

- Stand in front of them and ask the questions, as you present each option point either to the left or to the right

- Depending on their answer the players must jump either to the right or the left. (e.g. if they say banana they go left, pear right etc.)

- As they divide between left and right you will get to learn a little about the likes and dislikes of your group

Items required

☐ Would you rather list

Also available

Puzzles, Quizzes and Other Stuff
101 more things to do with children and young people

Tirzah l Jones
128pp, paperback
ISBN 978-1-84625-228-0

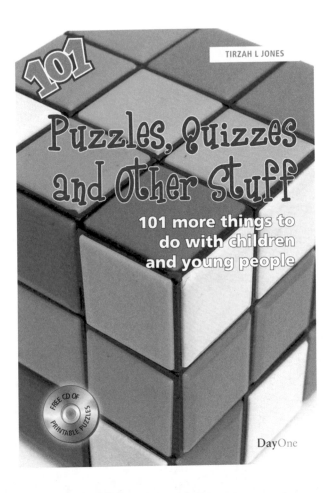

Games, games, more games!
101 great ideas for youth clubs

Tirzah l Jones
128pp, paperback
ISBN 978-1-84625-168-9

TIRZAH L JONES

Games, Games, More Games!

101 great ideas for youth clubs

DayOne

Crafts, crafts, more crafts!

101 great ideas for youth and children's clubs

Tirzah l Jones
128pp, paperback
ISBN 978-1-84625-228-0